page 130   page 92

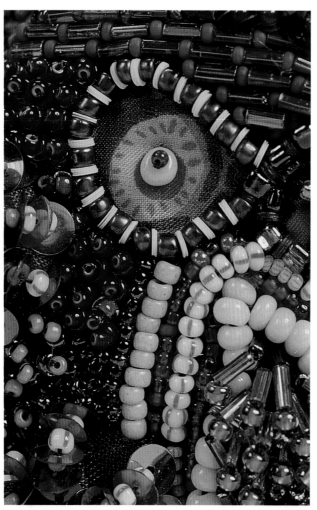

page 23

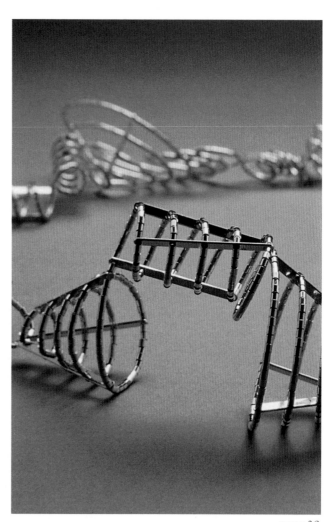

page 30

The Best in
Contemporary
Beadwork

Bead International 2000

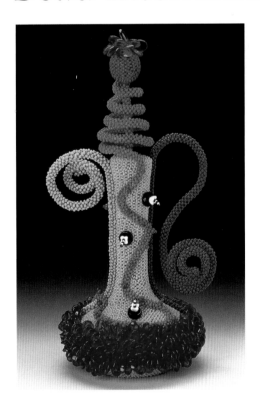

The Dairy Barn Cultural Arts Center
Co-produced by *Beadwork* Magazine

 INTERWEAVE PRESS

The Best in Contemporary Beadwork
Bead International 2000

Book Design by Elizabeth R. Mrofka
Edited by Jean Campbell
Cover artist Leslie Ciechenowski
Cover photograph by Larry Stessin

Copyright 2000, The Dairy Barn Cultural Arts Center
Photography copyright 2000, Brian Blauser

Interweave Press
201 East Fourth Street
Loveland, CO 80537
USA

Library of Congress Cataloging-in-Publication Data

The best in contemporary beadwork: bead international 2000/
co-produced by Beadwork magazine and the Dairy Barn Cultural Arts Center.

p.   cm.

Includes index

ISBN 1-883010-77-2

1. Beadwork—Exhibitions. 2. Glass beads—Exhibitions. I. Dairy Barn
Southeastern Ohio Cultural Arts Center. II. Beadwork (Loveland, Colo.)

NK5440.B34 B48 2000

745.58'2'074—dc21

00-025083
CIP

Printed in China at Midas Printing International
First Printing: IWP 7M:400:CC

Table of Contents

page 31

Susan Cole Urano
Director

When board member Mary Gates Dewey first brought the idea of an international bead show to the program committee of the Dairy Barn Southeastern Ohio Cultural Arts Center, we were skeptical. Actually, we thought she was crazy. How could bead art make a dramatic exhibition that would fill our 7,000 square feet of gallery space and attract visitors? As we began to investigate the work of contemporary bead artists, however, we were soon swayed; in fact, we became as enthusiastic as Mary was when she first presented the idea. And now, the Dairy Barn is proud to present its second international biennial bead art exhibition, *Bead International 2000*.

We have many to thank for this beautiful exhibition and book. Our new partnership with Interweave Press and editor Jean Campbell has produced this catalog. We thank Jean and her colleagues at Interweave for their help and support.

This year's jury consisted of David Chatt, NanC Meinhardt, and Kenneth Trapp. Their expertise brought laser-sharp insights to the process and the analysis of the field. We thank them for the many hours they devoted to selecting this year's show. We especially want to thank David Chatt for his thoughtful essay on the jury process in this catalog. Both emerging and established artists may find direction and tips for entering juried shows that will prove helpful in their careers. If not, it's always enjoyable to read David's writing.

The exhibition will leave the Barn this fall and travel for two years to museums in Illinois, Alaska, Arizona, and Michigan.

We are grateful to the major sponsors who have joined us in presenting *Bead International*: Miyuki Shoji Company of Japan, Byzantium of Columbus, Ohio, and The Ohio Arts Council. We also appreciate the support of The Athens County Convention and Visitors Bureau, the City of Athens, Larry Conrath Realty, The Athens Messenger, Beads & Things, and Julie Clark and all the Dairy Barn staff and volunteers who have made this project possible.

I invite you to come to visit the Dairy Barn during this or any other exhibition.

Susan Cole Urano
Executive Director

Cheryl Cobern-Browne
Foreword

The works presented in this show reflect the continued unfolding and maturing of an ancient art form as it evolves into a new era. The reader of these pages is invited to become lost in the beauty of color, form, and the movement of beads worked together. Each piece stimulates the viewer to take another look, to treasure the concepts conveyed in the work.

The "New Beadwork", as Kathlyn Moss and Alice Scherer so aptly deemed it a few years ago, is still quite new, but it is rapidly changing before our eyes. Beads are not necessarily for jewelry or adornment anymore; they have become sculptural elements for expressing life issues, the nature of relationships, and social concerns. They communicate abstract ideas and humorous ways of looking at life. As such, they have become a luscious and seductive medium for visual arts.

Two main points may be made about contemporary beadwork. One, artists are pushing beadwork's limits, extending the medium into new realms. Two, the world is learning to respect, understand, and get excited about beadwork's new boundaries. At The Bead Museum I am frequently asked about the history of beadwork. Where did our contemporary stitches originate? How far back can we trace beadwork? What kind of materials have been used?

Beyond the immediate answers I am able to provide, the overall answer is clearly that more study is needed; all materials that have not deteriorated must be carefully examined. We know that the ancient Egyptians made beads of faience, a precursor to glass. Broad netted faience collars were used extensively for ceremonial as well as for funerary costumes. It is interesting to note that Egyptian beadwork of ca. B.C. 300 is identical to netted peyote work.

A few ornate bead-encrusted ecclesiastical ornaments remain from the Middle Ages. In her book, *Glass Beads from Europe*, Sibylle Jargstorf tells us that eventually this fascinating style of beadwork was considered too worldly for ecclesiastics and such decoration was disapproved.

Valerie Hector has investigated the origins of European beadwork and tells us that the techniques of working with beads in many cultures closely resembles that of weaving with fibers; thus beading is truly an ancient craft. Her research of seventeenth century beadwork shows a form of continuous thread weaving that is similar to the popular stitches of today.

In North America, Natives used natural substances such as shell, bone, and porcupine quills for decoration until the traders of the 1700s introduced small glass beads, which subsequently dominated much Native craft.

Today, the glass bead industries of Europe, India, and now Japan produce vast quantities of beads for world consumption. The range of colors in the seed-bead industry has grown to astounding proportions, providing color palettes with a remarkable variety of hues and tones.

Contemporary beadworkers owe a great deal of thanks to the fine teachers of beadwork of this past decade. These individuals have shared their expertise, encouraged students, refined techniques, stimulated ideas, and instilled ethics. We cannot help being influenced by "others" work. We see something beautiful and it inspires us to create for ourselves. Not by copying, but by stretching someone else's ideas into new dimensions of our own. In just this way, the work in Bead International 2000 will stimulate beadworkers to shout in joyful creative voices of color and form. It will encourage everyone to participate in the magical exercise of combining beads, one by one, to create the quizzical, the representative, the obscure, the provocative, and, most certainly, the pleasing works of bead adornment.

Bead art commands a wider audience each year, finding respect and admiration in fields formerly resistant. Art teachers are using beads in schools; art galleries are exposing the public to quality bead workmanship. Thousands of talented housewives, professionals, and young people are taking up the hobby and finding solace and joy in the bounty of ideas possible with beads. The passion for this work is reflected in burgeoning class attendance at conferences, public events, and bead stores around the country.

The field bursts with energy; its horizons continue to expand. The amount of enthusiasm generated by today's beadwork stimulates teachers, students, and artists to try new things, to push the limits even further, combining stitches and techniques, mixing other media with beads. Beads can do it—like no other!

Itself a circle, the bead brings the heritage of antiquity to new life at the turn of this millenial century.

Cheryl Cobern-Browne
The Bead Museum
Glendale, Arizona

page 39

NanC Meinhardt
Juror

To submit your work to a juried beadwork exhibit is a big decision. After all, your piece is more than a collection of beads and time. Your work is the culmination of an involved creative process which is fraught with all of the artistic dilemmas inherent to such an undertaking. Most people, myself included, suffer moments of anxiety at the prospect of their work being "judged" in order to gain acceptance into the exhibit. Doubts arise: "Is my work good enough, will the jury see why my piece is special (it is certainly significant to me), is rejection or acceptance of my work a statement about the quality of my art, and what assurance do I have that the members of the jury are qualified to make such decisions?"

I wish it were possible to remove all uncertainty and provide straightforward universal answers to your concerns. Jurying art (or craft, as I do not separate the two outcomes; I see art as a verb, the activity of creating objects) is not absolute with fixed rules and reliable expectations. Rather, the jurying process is an extension of the making of art. Jurors are individuals with well-developed, yet purposefully diverse, backgrounds and aesthetic sensibilities, with open minds and often strong opinions who gather to make decisions about the composition of an exhibit.

The jurying process is, in actuality, an extension/continuation of the creative process. The pieces selected for exhibition are the jury's work of art created from a palette of submitted slides. The exhibit includes and transcends individual pieces.

The exhibition itself becomes an artistic experience expressing a combined aesthetic taste, spatial considerations, intriguing visual pleasures and challenges, creative surprises—in other words, an interactive viewing extravaganza of beadwork breathlessly waiting for an audience to arrive.

NanC Meinhardt
Beadwork Artist and Mentor

Sssssssnake

Kenneth R. Trapp
Juror

On August 27–28, 1999, David Chatt, NanC Meinhardt, and I juried Bead International at the Dairy Barn from slides submitted by artists. The experience was a real pleasure because it was well-structured and proceeded smoothly in predictable stages. The three of us worked well together. As the only non-practitioner on the jury panel, I must confess that without the guidance of the juror-artists I alone would have made some egregious mistakes; I would have accepted pieces that were unacceptable by the rules of the competition. This said, I do not believe eliminating non-practicing artists from art jurying is wise. It is, of course, hoped that all jurors are visually astute, have a seasoned and experienced eye, and can recognize artistic conviction in any medium.

In dividing the responsibilities for jurors' statements among us, I asked to discuss the importance of slides in juried competitions. The reason I asked to discuss the issue of slides is because Bead International was my third jurying experience in as many months. And in all three experiences the quality of the slides submitted became a major issue.

For a juror, the quality of an artist's slides is inseparable from the seriousness of the artist's commitment to art. Put simply, good slides separate the committed artist from the hobbyist. Why some artists believe it is acceptable to submit under- or over-exposed, out-of-focus, or dirty slides to jurors never ceases to amaze me. A juror should not have to second-guess an artist. A good slide should impart all necessary information that a juror must have to make an informed decision.

Slides should not be seen as a necessary evil but as an invaluable record. Slides are an artist's personal history and in some instances when art is inadvertently destroyed or its whereabouts unknown, a slide is often the only existing image and record. Good slides are a worthwhile investment, in spite of the cost. Quality does cost. But quality will last. There is no reason that quality slides and photographs will not last for decades.

I have heard artists say that "I can't afford to pay for good photography." My reply is: "You can't afford not to pay for good photography and expect your career to advance." Good photography is not a luxury but a necessity, the same way every writer needs an editor.

Why do I pay so much attention to the slides and not to the art? Let me begin with the obvious: to jury art from slides is to jury slides. The clearer, cleaner, sharper, and more straightforward the slide is, the easier and faster a juror can make an informed decision. To be sure, the presentation of art through slides leaves much to be desired. But until a better method of jurying comes along, we are left to deal with this imperfect system.

In the end, I hope a good slide can convey the artist's full success and intent. I look for integrity, self-confidence, conviction, competence, adventure, and a memorable experience in the art I jury from slides.

Kenneth R. Trapp
Curator-in-Charge
Renwick Gallery of the National Museum of American Art
Smithsonian Institution

David K. Chatt
Juror

In the Beginning

In 1987 I made an appointment with a women's accessory shop in downtown Seattle. I hoped the owner would consider carrying my jewelry in her store. By the late 1980s, I had been working with beads for a few years and I was really excited about some of my work. The jewelry I took to the store represented the very best pieces I had produced to that point.

Making that appointment meant I was committed to putting my heart and soul out on a table to be approved or rejected by the world at large, but I longed for the validation of having my work affirmed. I was positive that if my beadwork were displayed in that store alongside those belts and bags it would mean I had made it.

With great trepidation, I entered the store exactly at the appointed time. Nervous, and trying to become invisible, I stood by while a saleswoman chatted leisurely with her customer. I was beginning to think that I actually had succeeded at disappearing when finally the saleswoman dismissed the shopper, and turning to me, asked how she might help. "I have an appointment to show some jewelry to the store owner," I said. She was immediately bored with the conversation. Though she momentarily looked confused for some reason, her face quickly returned to boredom. "The owner's not here right now," she said. Then, nodding her head toward the rear of the store, "Why don't you just put your things on the table in the stock area. I'll be there in a minute."

I trudged off to the stockroom where she left me alone to lay out my life's work on a Formica tabletop while she proceeded to have a leisurely telephone conversation. I sat and waited for her, feeling my hair grow. Finally, she tore herself away from the front of the shop and headed in my direction, ready to deliver her opinions.

Coming through the door, she glanced at my jewelry and made a face that made me feel like a bad smell. It only took an instant for her to tell me that I was using "unfashionable colors." "And, you're silly to think this work is worth the prices you're asking!" she added. Dismissing me with a "Quit-being-a-nuisance-and-take-your trinkets-away" wave of the hand, she swept out of the stockroom, leaving a cloud of overpriced fragrance in her wake.

Now, years later, I look back on that experience and realize that I was in the wrong place, with the wrong product, and I was showing it to the wrong person. At the time, I was angry and hurt, but instead of proving the woman right, I became even more committed to my quirky sense of color. I raised my prices and started doing more non-wearables so that I wouldn't be forced into making only pieces that "reasonable, tasteful" people would wear.

As my career has developed, I have had many personal successes, immeasurably sweetened by the bitterness of that early encounter. I have also had a number of opportunities to sit in judgment of others' work. I will never do so without remembering how it felt to take my first steps out into the world, displaying my work for others to judge. As a teacher of beadwork and one of three jurors for this show, I am keenly aware that many of the images we reviewed represent the artist's first step out. Instead of remaining an anonymous entity, deeming your work acceptable or not, I have kept careful notes of the selection process in the hope that you will understand how and why we reached the decisions that we did. If you have ever wondered "why this piece?" or "why not my piece?" when visiting an exhibit, I hope this will help.

Selecting the Work

We three jurors began the process with 419 pieces to consider for inclusion in the show. Each artist was allowed to submit up to three pieces. The ideal number of selected works was 80.

We began reviewing images of the 419 pieces one Saturday morning. The identities of the artists were kept secret except when we recognized work that could only be from a particular artist or when we were presented with a piece that appeared to be "overly inspired" by another artist's work. In the former cases we were allowed to verify or ask for the identity of the artist. If a piece turned out to be "overly inspired" by the work of another, it was removed from further consideration.

The first run-through of the slides went fairly quickly and without any discussion among the three jurors. We looked at the work just long enough to form and record an opinion. We each had a list of the pieces we were all reviewing, including number, title, dimensions, and a space on the paper to record our vote. We were asked to give each piece a rating of one, two, or three. "One" referred to pieces that we would not consider further; "two" indicated work that we were unsure of and that we needed to see again; and "three" designated work that we felt sure we wanted to include in the show. Any piece that had a score of three at the end of round one was removed from further rounds. Any piece that had a score of eight or nine was set aside as a finalist. The rest of the images were reloaded into a slide carousel for the next run-through. At the end of round one, we had 40 finalists, 71 rejections, and 348 for further consideration.

Accordian Box

After another look at the images we had selected as finalists, we began round two. This round was again done with no discussion among the jurors other than the initial admonition that we were going to have to agree among ourselves to be more critical if we didn't want to see round 82!

In round two, a score of "five" or better was required for consideration in future rounds. Any piece with a score of "eight" or "nine" was set aside with the finalists. The results of round two were twelve additional finalists for a total of 52, and the elimination of 142 more pieces. This left 154 pieces for further consideration.

At this point, we decided to have some discussion among ourselves about the remaining work. This discussion was fairly polite and reserved, and the third run-through reflected our willingness to see the others' point of view. This particular approach to the process proved relatively fruitless, however. We were able to eliminate only an additional 22 pieces, meaning that we still had 120 finalists. We had to eliminate one-third of them. On that note, we broke for lunch.

After lunch, we resolved to make the hard choices. As one can imagine, these would become more difficult with each successive round.

I have to say

it was thrilling

to see all the work

together at once

and I am proud

to have my name

associated with this

collection of work.

First we added the finalists back into the group and took another look at all of the 120 pieces still under consideration. By now we starting feeling more comfortable with each other, and this fact made for much more colorful discussion. Opinions were offered up only to be blasted by the other jurors. We each took turns being alone in our enthusiasm, or lack thereof, for a particular piece. This interaction explains why juries consist of an odd number of jurors. After all the jurors have had an opportunity to air their opinions, and the vote is taken, it is impossible to become deadlocked. The majority wins.

In spite of the difficulty of the task before us, we were able to eliminate another 27 pieces in round four.

We still had to exclude 13 more pieces in round five. This process evoked stirring death-row appeals and poignant indictments. After major discussions, followed by some give-and-take, we actually made a preliminary agreement on the final pieces for the show. We decided to meet the next day for one last look at the accepted work and for the selection of awards.

Sunday morning, over breakfast, we decided to take one last look at all of the rejected works. We agreed that any juror would be allowed to make one final appeal to include any previously excluded piece. Likewise, we agreed to look through the accepted works and pull out any about which we were less sure. We also reviewed the catalog from the previous show and realized that a few pieces preliminarily accepted for this show were so similar to what the artist had submitted for the last show that we thought it might be better to reconsider them. We wanted to select work that would help this current show have its own identity.

It was our intention to encourage the artists who are stretching themselves, exploring new material. We wanted to give new artists an opportunity to show their work rather than to show the work of artists who had already shown similar work at this venue. This also gave us a bit of leeway for including back into the exhibit some of our previously-excluded favorites.

After the final run-through of all the work, we set the slides out on a light table and grouped them together. This gave us the opportunity to see if we were heavy or light in any particular area and to make the final adjustments.

At this point, we all had a good look at the show in its entirety, confirming that we had chosen a strong show that speaks well of the medium. I have to say it was thrilling to see all the work together at once and I am proud to have my name associated with this collection of work.

Do's and Don'ts for Juried Shows

Now that you've had a look at how arduous the process of selecting the work is, I want to talk about the reasons that some work is accepted in a juried show and other work is rejected.

1. Never submit a poor-quality slide. A great slide of an average piece is better than a lousy slide of a great piece. Slides should be documentary. Do not clutter up the image with a lot of extras. The image should show the work and as little else as possible. The image should show all of the work. Detail slides are for focusing in on a particular aspect of the work that may not be clear or that requires further explanation, but at least one slide should be of the whole piece and nothing but the piece. Even models can distract from the viewing of the piece. If you do decide to use a model, make sure you use a professional. To quote my fellow juror NanC Mienhardt, "If you are in the picture, get out!" (Kenneth Trapp writes more about slides in his juror's statement on page 11.)

2. Be aware of the overall look. Many works were rejected in this show because a decent piece was put into a poor-quality frame, or a stand or support system was devised as an afterthought. The frame or stand or clasp is part of the piece and is judged accordingly. Remember that every part of the piece is part of the piece. The functional aspects of the part should not distract the viewer in any way. One of my own ongoing pet peeves is clasps. Often an artist spends much thought and many hours creating a great wearable only to attach it to a closure device that has more to do with a factory in China than any statement that the artist had hoped to make.

3. It was difficult to tell on some of the considered works for this show if the artist was responsible for all of what we were seeing. I am thinking of one piece in particular that was nearly rejected because we were unsure whether the artist had created the beads used for the piece. The major focal point of the piece was the beads, so if the beads had been found and merely assembled it would not have been appropriate to include it in the show without the maker of the beads being credited. Finally, it was decided not to include the piece in the show until it was discovered that the artist had included a postcard, for notification, with a photograph of the piece on it, making clear the fact that the artist had, indeed, both created the beads and assembled them. Be clear in your descriptions. Tell the jurors what they are seeing.

4. Usually, it is not appropriate to exhibit work that is not completely of your own making, unless it is obvious that the design used is deliberately part of a statement that you are trying to make. Warhol's tomato-soup-can series is a great example of the preceding point. But as a juror, I am uncomfortable accepting work when I feel that a prominent part of the piece features a design that is not entirely that of the artist. If you have embellished a piece of fabric, who designed the fabric? If you have used a number of beads that are handmade, who designed the beads? This is not always a clear line to draw, but be aware that it is a concern when jurors are considering work.

5. It seems appropriate at this point to mention work that is reminiscent of a particular cultural tradition. It is hard for a jury to evaluate this kind of work in a show of contemporary work. Generally I think that traditional work should be done by those whose culture the tradition reflects, or by those who are exploring the traditions of a particular culture from an academic or historical perspective. In an anonymous jurying situation, traditional work is often not considered, even if it is being used in a contemporary way, because not enough information is available to the jury and also because the jury may feel unqualified to evaluate the work.

6. As jurors, we want each piece to have its own voice, so if there are several great pieces that are similar, only one may be chosen. Or, if the jurors think that the statement being made by a particular piece has already been made enough times in previous venues, we may opt not to use it at all. What is different or unique about your piece? What are you showing us that we have not seen before? Many people enjoy making and wearing necklace bags made from beads. There was a time when this was a new and interesting idea. Folks, that time has passed. You may still want to make one, you may still want to wear one, but from an exhibitor's point of view, that subject has just about been covered. We want work that is different from work that we have seen before, as well as different from other work in the show.

7. In a medium such as this, most of the work tends to be small. When choosing work, jurors want a variety of scale. A piece that is a giant by comparison to the size of other submitted work is going to have an advantage over a smaller piece.

8. Be aware of what you are trying to say with a piece and don't be distracted. Don't put all of your ideas into the same piece. Sometimes, as an artist, the process of creating becomes so private and self-serving that the viewer is left out of the experience. Some of the work that was rejected in this show was technically proficient but chaotic—too much embellishment, too many colors, too many beads fighting for attention. Some of that last comment relates to my own personal aesthetic sense, but it is really satisfying to see a piece that takes full advantage of the medium, the subject matter, and the vision of the artist, then stops before it becomes cluttered.

9. Where's the Beads? Always read your prospectus to be sure that your work fits the requirements. For this show there were many pieces that we felt were great pieces, but when the hard choices were being made, we had to refer back to the statement in the prospectus that asked for work in which beads were used as the primary medium and were of primary focus.

Final Comments

Choosing a collection of work to make an interesting and cohesive show is much more difficult than just choosing the best pieces or your favorite pieces. Each of the jurors had favorites that ended up with the rejected works. Our task was to select work that best illustrated the diversity and innovation taking place in a medium that is still defining itself in the world of contemporary fine craft.

Some of the pieces in this show speak of hours upon hours of commitment. In order to be able to produce a piece that is both technically proficient and artistically mature, one must spend infinite hours developing and perfecting technique and honing artistic vision.

The process of creation for most of these pieces happens at a speed so glacial it makes the word "spontaneity" seem like an oxymoron. Contrasting with the incredibly time-consuming and detailed efforts in this show is the work of some artists who chose to focus on the most literal definition of the word "bead," for the purposes of this exhibit, as "any pierced object." These works offer us scale and humor.

We wanted the show to be interesting to behold from a novice's point of view, as well as from the viewpoint of people on the front lines of contemporary beadwork. Any show with which I have ever been involved had a piece or two that was selected for what I call its "Hmmm" factor—the piece that people see and ponder. It is often the most controversial piece in the show and, invariably, it will be the favorite of some and the irritant of others. Controversy adds some tension to a show. It also provides a reference point for viewing some of the other works.

We, as a jury, endeavored to make choices that would reflect our commitment to diversity, excellence, fairness, and the future success of this medium. Above all, it is our hope that the statement these collected works make is one that will inspire you, as it has us.

David K. Chatt
Beadwork artist and teacher

Accordian Box

Gisela Arndt
Berlin, Germany
Day and Night, A Little Dream Town

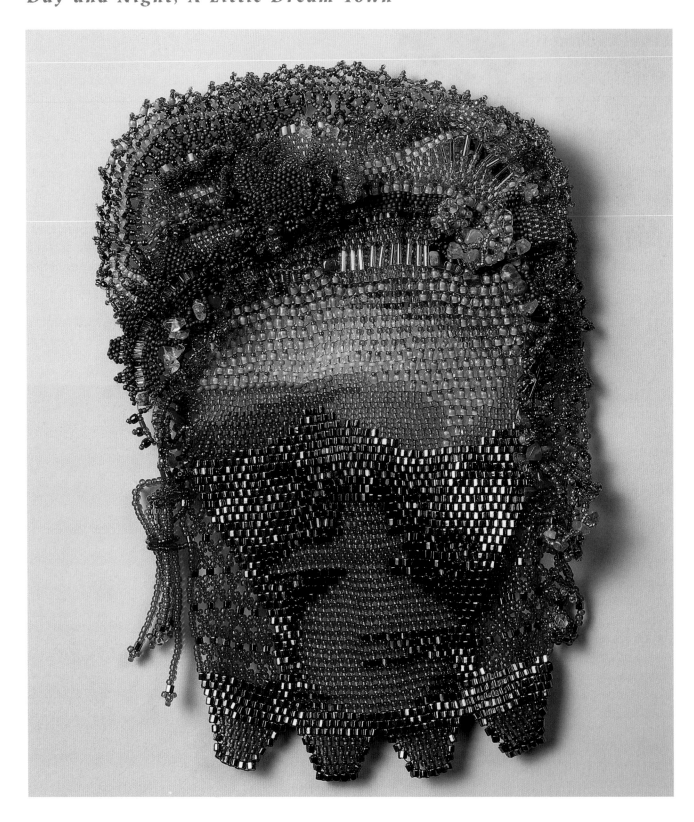

T his miniature is a three-dimensional picture, not something that you can wear like jewelry. It is a painting or sculpture. An expression of a romantic dream. It does not need an accurate explanation; each person can see something different in it.

Carolyn Prince Batchelor

Flagstaff, Arizona

Midnight

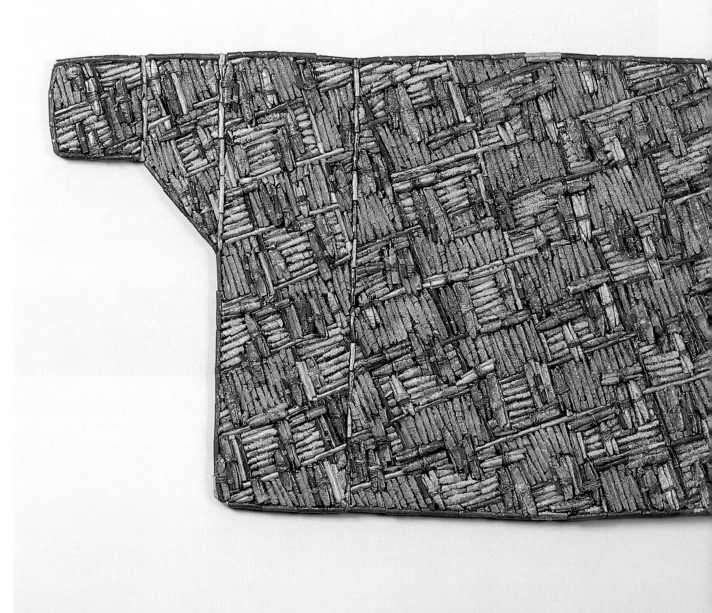

Carolyn Prince Batchelor

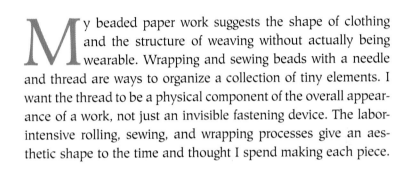

My beaded paper work suggests the shape of clothing and the structure of weaving without actually being wearable. Wrapping and sewing beads with a needle and thread are ways to organize a collection of tiny elements. I want the thread to be a physical component of the overall appearance of a work, not just an invisible fastening device. The labor-intensive rolling, sewing, and wrapping processes give an aesthetic shape to the time and thought I spend making each piece.

JoAnn Baumann
Glencoe, Illinois
Beaded for the Ball

The idea for this evening bag came while I was watching the opera *Madame Butterfly*. Perhaps the elegance of carrying such a bag to the opera is what first fueled the work, but as I plunged ahead, the bag became a challenging exercise in color exploration. It's composed of 200 intricately beaded balls; each bead and each beaded bead relates to its surrounding mates in subtle variation, a feast of form and color. While reflecting on the elegance of the finished creation, I was struck by the irony that, on another level, I was also seeing a huge beaded ball. A beaded ball composed of 200 smaller beaded balls sewn precisely in place to make one hell of a huge statement!

V ivid color, lush dense foliage, wonderful costumes, and spectacular under-water sights all combined to inspire this fanciful embroidered piece. I am inspired by my surroundings on trips to the Caribbean with my husband. He scuba dives and I sit in lush cabanas and bead. My need to interpret the beauty around me and the sights my husband sees while diving drove me to create this sumptuously colorful work. A textural piece, it combines wonderful Caribbean colors and a sea-like creation wrapped together.

Marianne Biagi
Chicago, Illinois
I Will-I Won't-I Do-I Don't

My husband said he wanted to separate. He's a cameraman and about two days later when he was hanging lights on the studio ceiling he stepped off the forklift and forgot how high he was. He caught his wedding ring on the lighting grip and ripped his ring finger almost off. He was hanging (and saved) by his wedding ring. The emergency doctors had to use metal snips to get the ring off. A few months later, he was fine, finger intact, and we had a stronger marriage by "talking it out". The rings say it all.

Karin Birch
Brunswick, Maryland
Untitled Heart

I spend as much time as possible in nature, where everything has a logic and beauty of its own. My work is often a response to those experiences. I am not interested in literal facts so much as emotional impact and the impression of my memory.

A.Kimberlin Blackburn
Kapaa, Hawaii
Garden Party, Kaua'I

My piece depicts a couple reveling in their garden. On a spiritual level, the female figure represents the Goddess with a fish on her skirt and her hands extending blessings. She is accompanied by the Green Man. He symbolizes a male nature element, vested in growing and nurturing green vegetative life.

Flora Book

Seattle, Washington

Cornucopia Neckpiece

I decided I would like to make individual beads out of thin silver tubing. I like working with anything with holes. As a young girl I was constantly stringing beads and now that I am 72 I still do the same thing but in an entirely different manner.

I had seen beads like these as a child when shopping with my mother. When I saw these paper beads again in Japan recently I had to buy them. It took a while before I could decide how to use them and finally this collar idea came to me.

Karen Bruner
Pasadena, California
Medusa

In Greek mythology Medusa was not always associated with horrific ugliness. She was once a beauty, attracting the attention of the Sea God Poseidon. When she found herself pregnant with his child, she entered his temple—a sacrilege. Her punishment was an ugliness that could turn a man to stone. Amazingly, the winged horse Pegasus sprang from her blood when she was killed. Never forget the beauty beneath the ugliest skin.

Robert Burningham

St. Paul, Minnesota

Etude in Black

Many kinds and sizes of beads were used in this piece. Each bead is either sewn down separately or sewn down six at a time with a small couching stitch placed between each bead. A variety of threads were used in the embroidery.

Beverly A. Carter
Surfside Beach, South Carolina
Udder Cream

I've been using this hand cream for years and have numerous empty jars filled with buttons and pins. When I began beading from my own ideas, the project was such a crazy idea I just had to do it. Once I found the cow it was pure joy from there on. The lid says, "I love this stuff!" with hearts and "Moo!" in the back.

Leslie Ciechanowski

Seattle, Washington

The House That Beads Built

he House That Beads Built was done over a six-month period. Its name tells of its "birth." It started as a sample piece for a class, but every time something was added it seemed to call for more. This process parallels the repeated addition of phrases in the nursery rhyme "This is the house that Jack built." This piece is an interactive piece, with the child on the swing and the roof that moves to reveal a mother who is watching her children from inside the house. In a way, the piece is about women's isolation, and their "invisibility" in society while raising children; hence you see the mother and child only dimly through the glass.

PHOTO BY LARRY STESSIN

Zamboodo Dancer is a playful and whimsical piece inspired by my daughters' love of dancing and swirling and by the bright colors and shapes of author/illustrator Dr. Seuss. It is meant to brighten one's spirit during the dark and gloomy winter months. The swirling coils imitate moving arms, the flounced "skirt" suggests a Spanish dancer, and the colors and coiled neckpiece reflect an African influence.

Ann Citron
Alexandria, Virginia
Offering

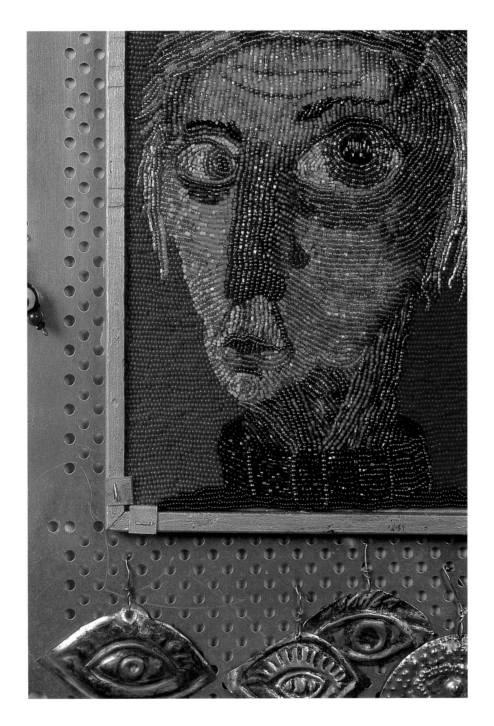

About four years ago, I suffered some damage to the retina of one of my eyes, affecting my vision. This piece is based on the idea that votive offerings depicting the injured limb or body part, can, along with supplications, induce the gods to restore the health or the use of the injured or impaired organ.

Sonya Y. S. Clark
Madison, Wisconsin
Beaded Prayers

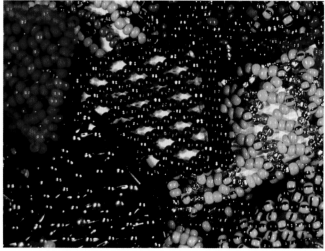

Inspired by the amulet prayer packets found throughout the African Diaspora and the shared etymology of the words "bead" and "prayer," I created beaded prayer packets of the written wishes, hopes, and dreams of my family and friends. This has lead to a larger undertaking, *The Beaded Prayer Project*, in which a variety of people are invited to create prayer packets to be displayed en masse.

This piece deals with communication, childhood, and hairstyles. When I was a child I was told that if you received a phone call in a dream you would be contacted by a special guardian. I was told these sort of tales by women who combed my hair into elaborate hairstyles.

Cynthia Coté
Calumet, Michigan
Blue Dress

I refer to my beadwork as "picture making." Although I have been working with beads for thirteen years, it took me ten to discover what I really wanted to do with the medium. One of my very early (and unlikely) bead mentors, a friend who is a folk artist, said to me as he watched me working a feeble little design on a piece of cloth, "Don't be a wimp, fill it in!"

Joan Dulla
Chandler, Arizona

67,983

On this piece I've shown the roots of a tree connecting to the stars which feed the tree to make leaves. This is my way of saying we all need to connect to exist.

As a metalsmith, I felt that the masculine characteristics of nuts needed to be met by the feminine ones of beading. Thus the nut cup.

JoAnn Feher
Seattle, Washington
Made Marion-ette

As a knitter, I never hoarded yarn. As a sewer, I bought fabric as I needed it. Seed beads are different. They have the appeal of small jewels or tiny candies. I take pleasure in having them near me. I am amazed what I can create with them. They talk to me, and things go well when I listen.

My work reflects my happiness when I bead. It is light and whimsical in nature. I hope that it will bring a smile and warm feelings to those who view it.

Linda Fifield

McKee, Kentucky

Blue Echoes

Artistic commitment is a way of life for me, and my family's tradition of craftsmanship is an invaluable part of my Appalachian heritage. Generations of women in my family have made handwork an integral part of the daily rhythms of life, and twenty-five years of experimentation with various on- and off- loom weaving techniques has let my skill mature. I turn wooden vessels on a lathe and cover them with precise, intricate stitches. The skill, patience, and commitment necessary to create these beaded vessels sustains my creative life.

Anne M. Fletcher
Tucson, Arizona
Beaded Rock

For me, beads offer an incredible pallet of color, shape, and texture. I find myself constantly thinking of new things to try. I like creating a fanciful, colorful piece that can be seen across the room but still holds surprises when examined closely. Texture is as important to me as visual appearance. I like the freedom and excitement of starting with only the sketchiest plan and letting the beads dictate the final outcome. Seeing a special bead or type of bead and then picking a technique or even inventing a technique that will show it off is challenging and fun. For me, knowing how a pattern structure works is as important as creating the actual piece.

Susan Etcoff Fraerman
Highland Park, Illinois
Bound for Glory I, II, & III

As a teenager, I spent five post-operative months bound in long-leg plaster casts. I found comfort in my imagination, particularly the daydream that one day I would saunter about in sublimely stylish high-heeled shoes.

In 1998, the American Council of Fashion Designers awarded the Stiletto Award for a shoe called by many "the limousine shoe" on the assumption that one can wear it only if no walking is required. We have not moved far from the sixteenth century when Venetian ladies wore such high platform shoes that they required the support of a servant. Yet, the special magic of shoes still fascinates.

Vanessa Galloway
Tucson, Arizona
Virgin of Guadelupe

The influence of Mexican culture has made the Virgin of Guadelupe a Southwest icon. She is the Virgin Mary as witnessed by Juan Diego on Tepeyac Hill in Mexico in 1531. Her presence is felt from the street to the church, from living rooms to grocery stores. She resounds further into the community, where she is seen as a goddess and as an ever-loving mother figure. She deserves to be beaded. This piece is based on the original, believed to have appeared on Juan Diego's tilma and remains intact today.

These ancient Roman glass beads are also known as "Diggem" beads. Once traded profusely, they are not as rare as one might expect. From my understanding, they're found in African soil, sometimes without even digging, being most noticeable after a rain. Their style and patina, plus the place and method of discovery, are evidence of their age.

Men Digging for Beads is an analogical piece where the bead has become larger than life. In the hot African sun men take a moment to pause before beginning their work of excavating a piece of history.

Beth P. Gilbert

Buffalo Grove, Illinois

Lox and Bagel (or Boy, Can I Cook!)

Beth P. Gilbert

As an artist, I move between two worlds, those of quilting and beading. Both disciplines depend on clarity of design, a good sense of color, and workmanship. My beadwork is generally joyous, reflecting a pure love of sparkle, translucence, texture, and color. I find beads very seductive and I attempt to draw viewers into my work by appealing to their sense of beauty. I love holding beadwork in my hands and watching it take shape as it develops a life of its own.

Laura Goldberg
Highland Park, Illinois
Mirror, Mirror...

B eading is a rhythm, a harmony. I generally work without a preconceived plan. When I'm on a "streak" the beadwork flows without much thought. I wish writing an artist's statement flowed as easily!

Peg Gyldenege
Puyallup, Washington
The Amazing Walk to Womanhood

Color has always been my companion. The discovery of beads changed my life forever. The magic begins when the small bits of color join the ideas that spill from my dreams. Time speeds by while I work and I often wonder if the clock is broken. How could so much time have slipped by?

Countless teachers have shared the secrets of beads with me. I wish to thank them all for initiating me into the wonderful world I now find myself a part of. Discovering others who share the passion has been an added bonus traveling this road.

Patty Haberman
Tempe, Arizona
Watch For Snakes in the Grass

My work is narrative and often autobiographical. I make sculptures that give a hint or fragment of a story, phrase, or event that I find interesting or humorous. Working with beads and their intense colors, weight, tactile qualities, and ability to reflect light is a sensual and rewarding experience. Stitching beads into three-dimensional objects by combining individual units to make a whole is a very labor-intensive and obsessive activity that I enjoy.

I wanted to make a sculpture that would incorporate chain mail and bead elements. Here I show a Seeker clothed in chain mail and beads. Chain mail represents protection and strength, and the openly woven beads represent the value of the free exchange of ideas. The beads allow some vulnerable areas to exist in the protective armor in which the Seeker surrounds himself. The Frog, offering a flower, represents the best that life can give. I hope that in the rush of the future we will still be able to be courted by frogs and realize what the best things in life are.

Susan Hillyer
Dublin, California
A Breath of Spring

I have always looked for meaning in life, and longed for my own life's work to be meaningful. As I discovered my passion for beadwork, I came to feel connected to other needlework artists past, present, and future, especially women. For all of history, women have worked with their hands and souls transforming bits and pieces of things into objects of beauty. It is a glorious thing to be living in a time when the "bits and pieces" are objects of beauty in their own right, and when the transforming with our hands and souls is recognized as art.

Mimi Holmes

Minneapolis, Minnesota

No Babies for Me, #3: Heartson

This is the third in a series of (I hope) nine banners to deal with the finality of my decision not to have children; not to use my body for that biological function. *Heartson* is a cross section of a fetal heart at four weeks.

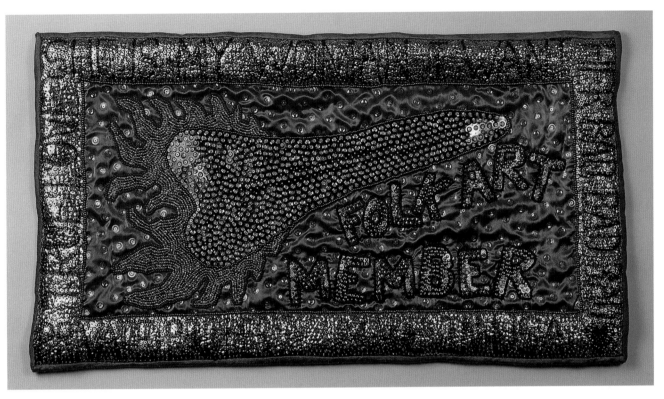

Folk Art Member is a bead and sequin version of a painting I did based on a drawing of a long-ago sweetie with whom I had a long-distance relationship. An artist himself, he accompanied his letters with drawings of flying members and comments around the border. I found this funny and touching at the same time.

Jihye Kim
Chicago, Illinois
Constructing Self. Shifting Self. Horizontal Self

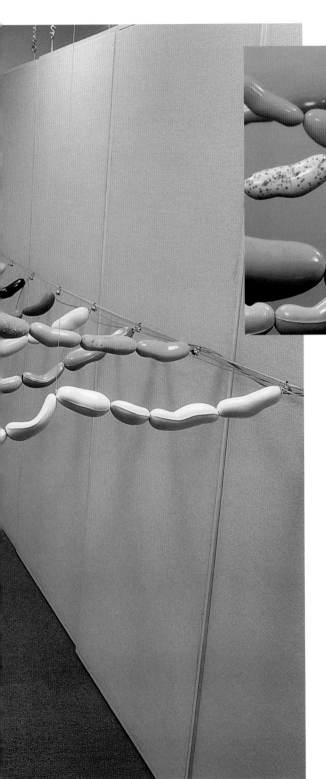

This installation, *Constructing Self. Shifting Self. Horizontal Self,* is about searching for female subjectivity without suppressing female sexuality and desire. The three-part title reflects the multiple meanings of the piece. "Constructing Self" means that I have been constructed and am still being constructed. "Shifting Self" means that there are many subject positions one inhabits, since one is not just a single being. "Horizontal Self" opposes horizontality to phallic verticality. The place that I want to create is a place of openness to which viewers can add their own experiences and feelings, their own lives, and create their own meanings. I hope my pieces stir emotions, inspire strength, and give pleasure.

Katherine M. Korff

Fort Gratiot, Michigan

The Burning Bush Liturgical Stole

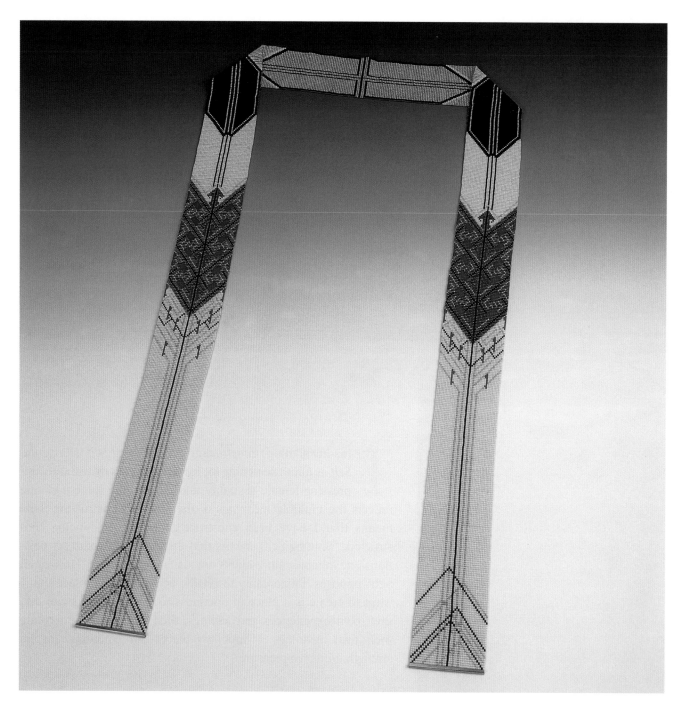

While the visual image of the burning bush holds a strong religious connotation, it has become for me an organic symbol of creative spirit. The passion that enriches the act of creating is ignited by an idea, continues to flame through the process, and, rather than being consumed by the fire, endures.

This sculpture represents wings and plays with movement from the front view and the two side oscillating lines. I use movement as a plastic art expression. The movement is activated mechanically and viewers can graduate the speed of the flight. They can walk around the sculpture and interpret different points of view: sideways "cleaning" is needed first, and from the front view it is now possible to fly. With this game I pretend to provoke different interpretations.

PHOTO COURTESY OF THE ARTIST

John w. Lefelhocz

Athens, Ohio

Gecko Cruiser

This bike was made to capture the kid in us. I wanted to catch the amusement, the speed, and the feel of how moving on air felt when riding a bicycle as a youngster. The gecko further represents these qualities—playful, lively, and acrobatic. The more you look the more you see. Thanks, Maxine.

This embroidery began as a guide to me as I built a labyrinth with forty-nine friends in my small town. She then grew into an embroidery.

Laura Leonard
Minneapolis, Minnesota
The Mother-In-Law Cometh

My art is about simple everyday life . . . those moments of whimsy and playfulness that seemed to be everywhere when I was a girl. Some might say it's a cross between realism and cartoons, but it's just the way I see the world.

Haley Licata
Highland Park, Illinois
Growth

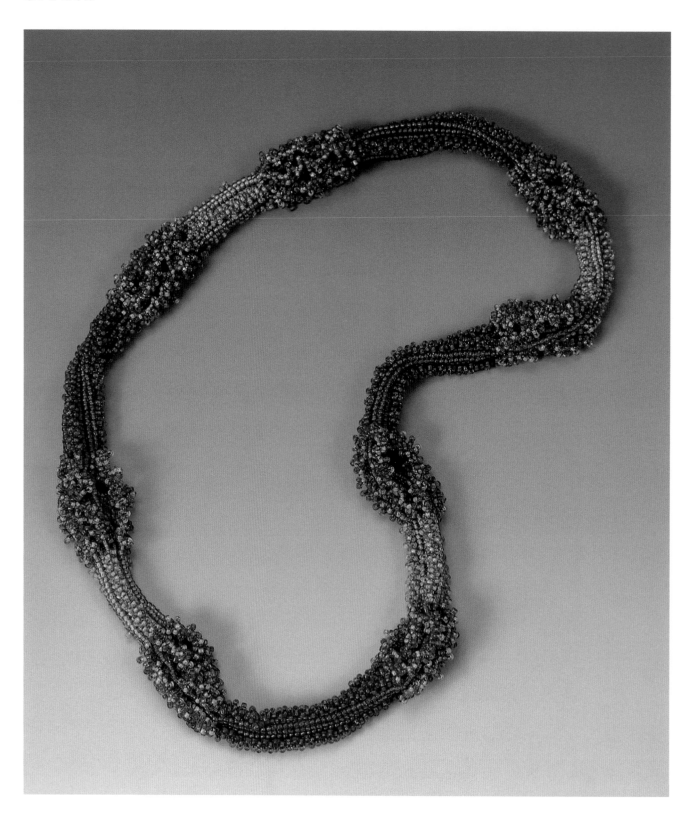

A rt has always been a creative outlet for me. From drawing with waxy crayons as a toddler to stitching beads as a teen, I have found that art is the constant variable in my life. Art is the direction that life has naturally taken, and this path has led me into the world of beads. I love the sculptural, tangible nature of beads as well as their colorful visual stimulation. My piece is entitled *Growth*, partly because of its organic nature, but mainly because of the growth I made in my own development as a bead artist.

Donna L. Lish
Clinton, New Jersey
Yellow Quake

Donna L. Lish

I adore the progression inherent in beading as one element is added at a time. The process mirrors experiential synthesis where I am continually strategizing, imaging, and always planning the next step on a given work.

I pursue sculptural forms that capture my thought process, my emotion, at the moment of origin. And, because the process is adaptive to diversions and refinement as I build each piece, it allows for those refinements and revisions as the problem solving evolves.

Eleanor Lux

Eureka Springs, Arkansas

To Digger

Lately, some of my work seems to take on a life of its own, something I don't have control of any more, and as I continue to work, I say to myself, "What is this?" Life moves on. There seems to be no answers.

My neighbor's dog, Digger, barked every thirty seconds until my neighbor returned from work. In an effort to win Digger over, I would bring her a treat every day, but she would only eat it when I was out of sight. Finally one day, she looked up at me, smiled, and gobbled up the cheese.

That weekend, my neighbor had her put to sleep. She said Digger had lost her energy, and didn't seem to care about living anymore. She figured Digger either had a heart condition or cancer. Life moves on. There seems to be no answers.

As I worked on this piece, I thought a good bit about Digger. She's dead now. Life moves on. There seems to be no answers.

Celeste Marafino
Stuart, Florida
The Snowbird

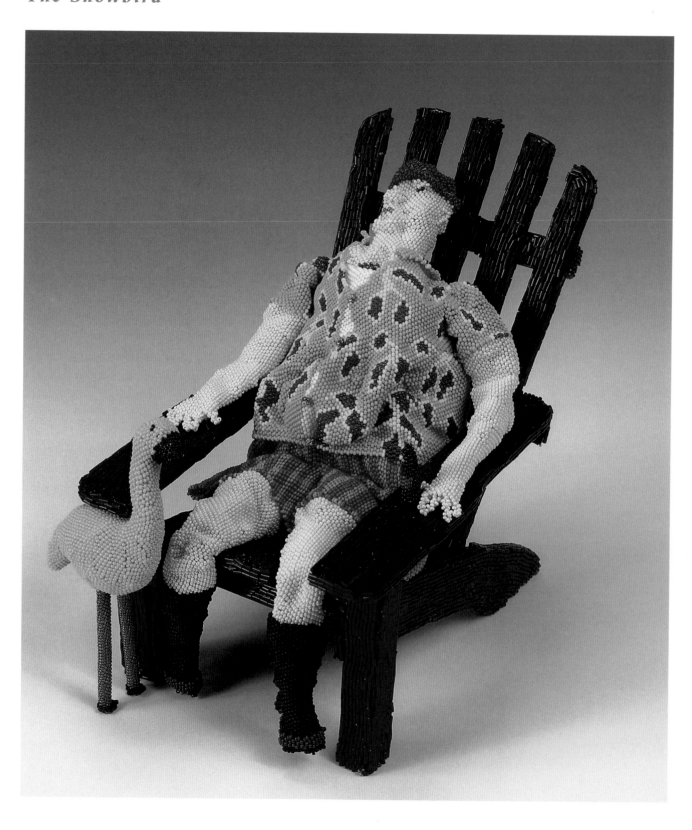

I 've been involved for many years in the field of art, specifically in oil painting and sculpture. Through these materials I have enjoyed creating with a wide spectrum of color and texture. When my interests expanded to beading, I soon realized the limitless possibilities for creation in this medium.

Of the various designs I have worked with beads, characterizations have piqued my interest at this stage of my work. *The Snowbird* has been a comical extreme for me. It reflects the light-hearted attempt made by people to escape the confines and conformities of their working life.

Deneen Matson
Highland Park, Illinois
Kimono #1

I have chosen to give off-loom bead weaving a unique application by creating a series of small-scale historically-based ethnic dress. My ultimate responsibility is to the original creators of the ethnic dress I choose to translate into beads. My challenge is to create a piece in beads as unique and beautiful as its cloth counterpart. Completing a piece that looks, acts, and feels like my initial vision is my greatest pleasure.

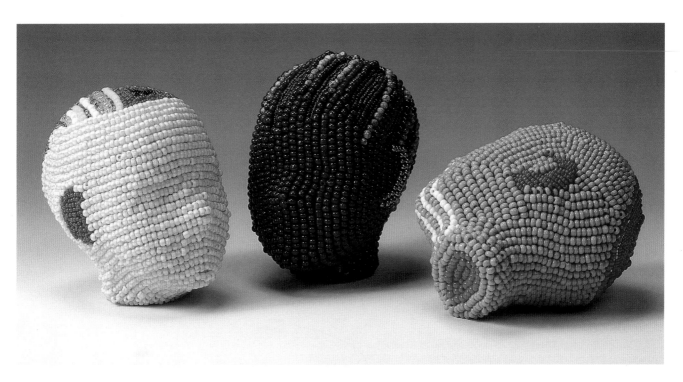

M y beaded doll heads reflect the basic primal feelings we humans exhibit toward representations of the human body, particularly when seen in three dimensions. Humans have made dolls since prehistoric times—for play and for more serious purposes of spiritual significance and instruction. This work speaks of the connection to those times.

Ann Tevepaugh Mitchell
Wayland, Massachusetts
Bathing Beauty #1

The idea began during a visit to California when I found a piece of wet sea kelp on a beach, naturally coiled in a wavy shape. After drying the kelp and allowing it to stabilize, I tried to express through beadwork the complexity of ocean light, using the kelp to create the movement. The figure pairs beadwork with glass, without either disguising the glass or being restricted to its shape. It uses the glass as part of its anatomy. The beadwork beyond the torso of the figure is wholly self-supporting and hollow, built without any inner structure. I used a shell and abstracted the face to symbolize the experience of merging with the elements of the ocean.

Nicole Nagel

Snowmass Village, Colorado

Spongo

Comically interstitial, my work does not acknowledge allegiance to either beadwork or sculpture. Set somewhere between fashion and funk, these offbeat objects challenge our ideas of what can become a bead. Meticulously beaded from materials foreign to the process, my objects are at once instantly recognizable but slightly strange. These images under subjection of our definition are familiar yet they verge on becoming nothing in particular. It is within this nonsensical area where I wish to place my work. The intersection where I hope they can become reliant on themselves.

Annisac

Lisa Niforos
Fort Lee, New Jersey
Red Bead on Canvas

Lisa Niforos

This intense study of pattern and color is the culmination of my passion for beadweaving and my exploration with the hot-glass fusion of these weaving techniques. Each part was sewn together piece by piece, like a quilt, taking over eighteen months to complete. The beaded fabric comprises five different patterns. By manipulating the opacity and transparency of the beads, I achieve a different look in each design. They are transformed, once again, when I bring these weavings to the kiln. These methods of working are very distinct and separate; however, in this opposition I find harmony. I am roused by the challenge of combining these thick, heavy pieces of glass with the fabric-like drapery of the beadwork. I pursue an activity between each separate component within the piece; their infusion creates energy united in the piece's totality, one solitary red bead.

Colleen O'Rourke
Chicago, Illinois
Loretta's Night In

W e bought our first house in 1998. The neighbors to the north are Loretta and Jerry, both in their seventies. Loretta was born in that house and has never lived anywhere else. They know the entire history of the neighborhood and the neighbors. She walks their dog, Maggie, at precisely the same times everyday, in her various housecoats. Tragically, their only child drowned at the age of 22, they have no family left, and most of their friends have passed away. She told me that I was lucky to have a hobby that I enjoy (beading) and that "one can only clean so much".

Sharon Peters
Alameda, California
Recycling at Daisy's Dairy

I made my first bead on the torch in April 1996, and was in turn burned, delighted, and hooked. Working with glass and flame is so much fun, it should be illegal. I like playing with primary colors and sculptural forms. My favorite pieces are bright, silly, tell a story, and make people laugh. The process of melting and forming the glass is so calm and meditative, and the gratification is so instant, that the finished piece is just an added bonus. Most of my beads are bright, cartoon-like, titled with bad puns, and many are one-of-a-kind.

Christy Puetz
East Bethel, Minnesota
Magestic Boil Suit

My dolls are miniature examples of real life—with a big butt. Using beads increases the visual appeal and also adds a hepatic quality to the doll's shape.

Articulated metal jewelry for the human neck usually takes the form of links, as in a chain, or as sets of beads. The manufacturing process is, naturally, repetitive. Patterns may be developed using differing shapes and sizes of links or beads. In this set of sterling silver beads, I have used a simple pattern of sphere/cylinder/sphere/cylinder and then disrupted it near the middle with a reel.

Ruth Marie Satterlee

Seattle, Washington

Barren By Choice

For many years I did not make art of any kind, I was too busy building a career. I thought about that choice during the time I created this piece, and saw that the barren time was a gift now and that I had willingly chosen career over art and raising children. The barren time fueled the desire to create so that it can't be extinguished now. After traveling through the stark beauty of the desert, the flowers in the oasis are all the more beautiful.

M*iss Fortune* is part of a series of shrines. They're united by an overall architectural design, images of ascending ladders, and a dichotomy of light and dark on each side. My shrines might be icons of an illusory religion or a reminder to find the sacred in everyday life. This piece began as a shrine to gambling—when the bride found her way in, it was named after her.

Carol Shelton
Columbus, Ohio
Beads Inside Hollow Holey Beads

My primary motivation in creating original pieces is aesthetic. But the new medium of polymer clay offers abundant opportunities to develop innovative techniques. For me, there is a strong focus on geometry and the mechanics of construction. I often make the clay do something it hasn't done before, working on the edge of disaster and making pieces that won't survive the construction process. On the other end of the continuum, I build pieces that are durable and develop innovative finishing techniques. Color and its interplay with light are also important. I use high contrast as well as subtle tones and shades.

Susan Socotch

Bowling Green, Ohio

Mardi Gras

Susan Socotch

Mardi Gras was my second beaded appliqué, attempt that evolved into a total experiment and challenge. Midway through this piece, I realized something needed to be done with the back of the fabric to stabilize it. I also work with plaster gauze and decided to experiment with the gauze on the back of the piece. I feel it was successful in not only giving the piece stability but also covering all the stitches on the back.

Susan Socotch
Bowling Green, Ohio
Impromptu

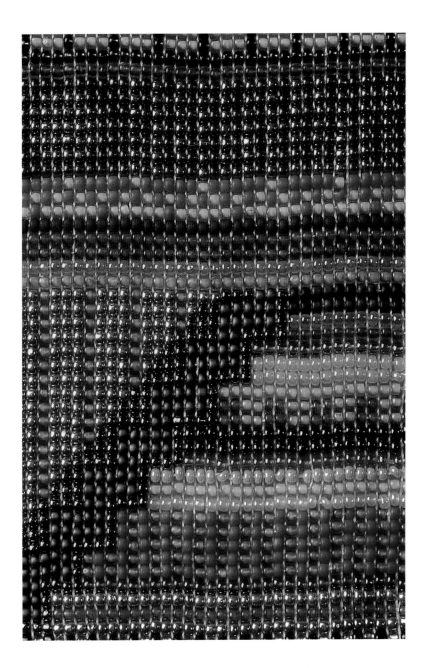

*I*mpromptu is just that. I had no pre-conceived plan of how I wanted this piece to turn out. Each section of color and pattern just happened. I thoroughly enjoyed creating this piece because of the freedom of adding an angle or a "texture" wherever I wanted; it was almost like drawing with beads.

Anne M. Solis

Memphis, Tennessee

Necklace of the Three Graces: Good Cheer, Splendor and Myth

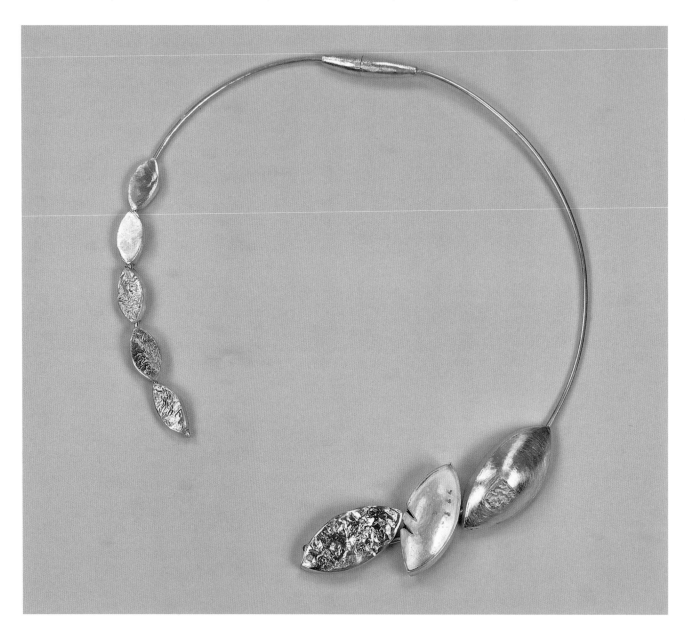

I am fascinated by the potential of three-dimensional vocabulary and language. I enjoy the challenge of transferring thoughts and ideas by three-dimensional means that are incapable of expression through verbal means. It's like making sense of a dream that escapes you or understanding a fleeting incomprehensible thought, and then bringing that dream or thought into a tangible form and refining it so that it can be justified among all the concrete things around us. It's stretching the boundaries of what we know and believe in order to introduce new thoughts and ideals to exist among the mundane.

Susan Sontag

St. Louis, Missouri

She Cannot Create Because She Cannot Feel

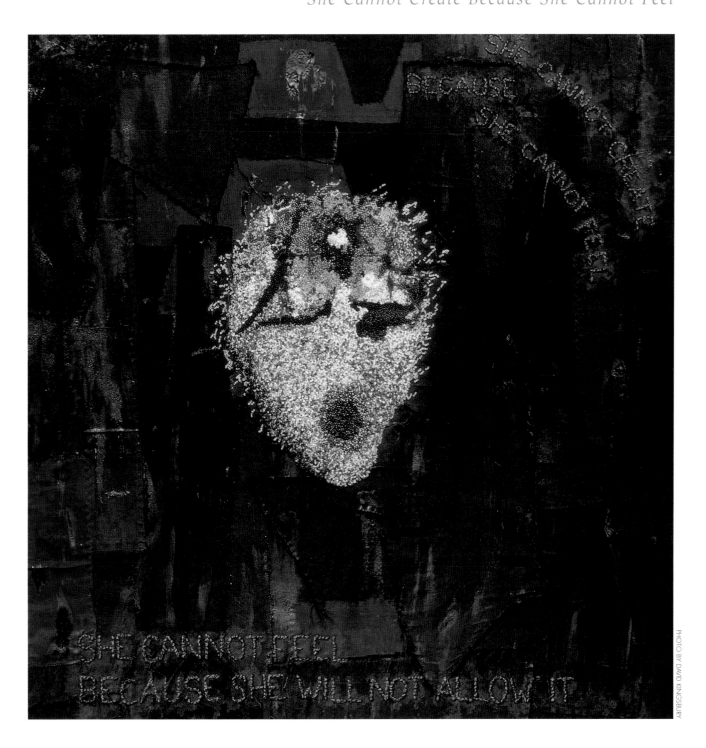

Years of arts administration has left this non-producing artist sliding on (white-hot) thin ice.

Fran Stone
Portland, Oregon
Synthesis

I came to this work as a creative outlet late in life. For myself I made the word "retirement" a misnomer. My life took on a new meaning because I was able to unlock my appreciation of color, texture, and shape in this medium. I am bursting with ideas and I believe that is what keeps me young. I am fortunately able to travel and view other societies in the way they translate their environment into adornments. This in itself gives me pleasure and enables me to be stimulated. Not only the process but the gratification of finishing a piece is an exhilarating experience.

Now that I am 75 years old, it seems that I still enjoy discovery in the beauty around me. I am most fortunate in finding this way to express myself.

Marcie Stone
La Mesa, California
Twilight

W orking with a palette of beads and threads, I make spontaneous choices that evolve into biomorphic syntheses of colors and textures. I am fascinated with the way the different beads play against each other, creating jeweled encrustations influenced by primitive art and organic forms.

Teresa Sullivan

Portland, Oregon

Feng (Abundant Harvest)

"Feng" is Chinese for "abundance". After first grouping the components by color, I saw a theme take shape. The large disk shows three animals playing cards and reads "stop monkeying". The beetle, revered by the ancient Egyptians, keeps the world intact by rearranging little piles of dung. A whirling-dervish arm, a snake vertebrae, and the meandering trails of beads suggest constant activity. Amber beads recall wheat, honey, beer; terra cotta red and black beads and objects summon earth and sweaty labor. Beadwork itself gives evidence of the importance of tiny, sustained movements.

James Edward Talbot
Austin, Texas
Fully On #2

My ultimate focus is the expression of magic. I favor materials that are luminous, sensual, richly colorful, and visceral, and I combine or layer them in unexpected, sometimes mysterious, sometimes exotic, sometimes playful ways. Always, my intent is to move people deeply, to ennoble, enlighten, or uplift them; to appeal to their highest, most magnificent selves; and to offer fresh glimpses, both of the reality around them and of their own wondrous natures. I want to take them above their daily distresses, be they familial, political, or cultural, and to show those distresses as something not really essential.

Sherri J. Thompson
Seattle, Washington
Litany (Ghosties and Ghoulies)

From the Middle and Old English words for prayer and rosary bead comes our word, bead. The association of beads with prayer appears in many cultures and religions, including a Catholic rosary or a Buddhist mala. For me, the time spent stitching beads together is a meditative and spiritual process.

This old Scottish litany was my favorite prayer as a child and this piece is an exploration of the bead/prayer connection, and of the power of words.

"From ghosties and ghoulies and long legged-beasties and things that go bump in the night, Good Lord, deliver us."

Marya LeMieux Vafaei-Makhsoos
Minneapolis, Minnesota
Prayer for COBAKA

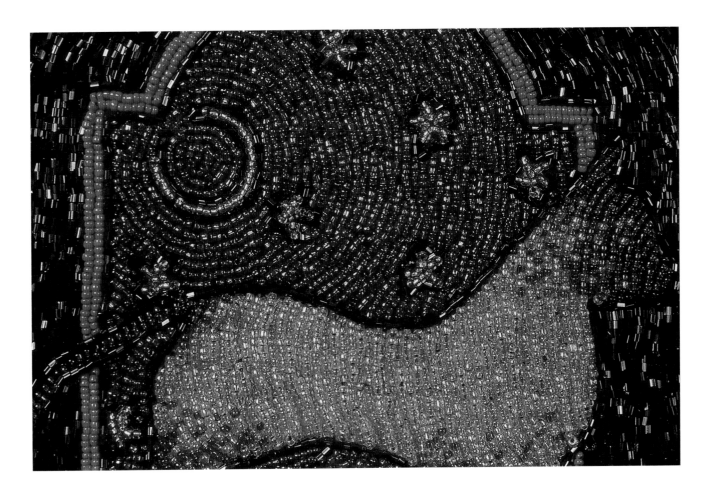

This work is a fusion of my love for religious icons, beads, and my mourning for my dead cat. Um...that came out wrong. Hmmm . . . This was my first attempt at backstich on paper. I had previously believed paper to be too flimsy and likely to tear but found canvas paper to be strong. I painted on the image in acrylic before beading, using the painting as my guide for colors and the brush-strokes as my guide for bead direction. Originally, I meant to frame this under glass but found viewers want to touch it, so I reinforced the back with glue and backed it with felt so it may be touched.

Sue Eckman Von Ohlsen
Chesapeake, Virginia
One Alcoholic's Life: A Tangled Web

The alcoholic has built a tangled web of lies and deceit in order to support the addiction. As the alcohol flows, it becomes first tears and then blood, which symbolize the pain, destruction, and ultimately death caused by the addiction.

Sally Wassink
San Francisco, California
Aren't We All Divine?

In all of my work (fiber and loomed beadwork), I like to tell a story and attempt to give each piece layers of meaning that may not be apparent at first glance. Beads are especially conducive to this idea because the element of light adds change. Images and colors that may have been hidden suddenly become visible.

Kay Whitcomb
Rockport, Massachusetts
Cloisonné Enamel Bead Choker

I have developed these cloisonné enamel beads since 1979. I've taught the technique through Enamel Guilds all over the United States and Tokyo. It is an American version of the Japanese-style cloisonné, which is placed on a vertical surfaced object using the wire work in an enamel flux. There are many challenges because silver wires can sink into the copper and cause eutectic firing. The silver gasses in the firing at 1500 F°, taking the color out of many pinks and lavenders. The challenges can be exciting goals; for pliqué à jour, this method is the ultimate direction!

Michelle Williams
Wilmette, Illinois
Untitled #1

I have been working on the idea for this piece for four years. It is an outgrowth of my more delicate work with seed beads, also based on the human form. Using bottle tops encrusted with beads is intriguing to me.

My initial goal was to create a large-scale installation piece for a gallery space. I like the idea of precious beads used on a grand scale. This piece, like all my work, created new challenges. I was forced to explore new materials and solve structural problems in new ways. It was fun, meditative, and freeing to create.

R*odman Dinka* was conceived and first based on a modern-day celebrity. It then took on a life of its own. I am always inspired by African costumes and beadwork. The sculpture began to take on African characteristics and it was transformed into a Dinka tribesman. Inside is a crystal that emanates positive energy to the viewer. This piece was a study for a larger piece that probably will not be executed.

Many of my images come from things I see on late night walks or drives. Some are scenes I see with my eyes closed. I specialize in nighttime versus daytime land-scapes because even the most mundane things become numinous and lovely in the selective illumination of urban night. I use glass beads to paint these pictures because the beads' colors and finishes are so intense, so full of presence. The more saturated the color, the more varied and sparkling the surfaces of the beads, the closer I get to the way my mind's eye sees.

Neva Wuerfel

Chandler, Arizona
Basic Bead Kit Bracelet

Art is a journey of internal discovery. Physically, I work to advance my technical skills, but mentally I strive to explore the relationships between concepts and methods. I am intrigued by the humorous and incongruent use of objects. Subtle connections between disparate ideas or situations are also fascinating. While thread is necessary to the process, an image is held together, most importantly, by its idea.

Neva Wuerfel
Devious Dipper

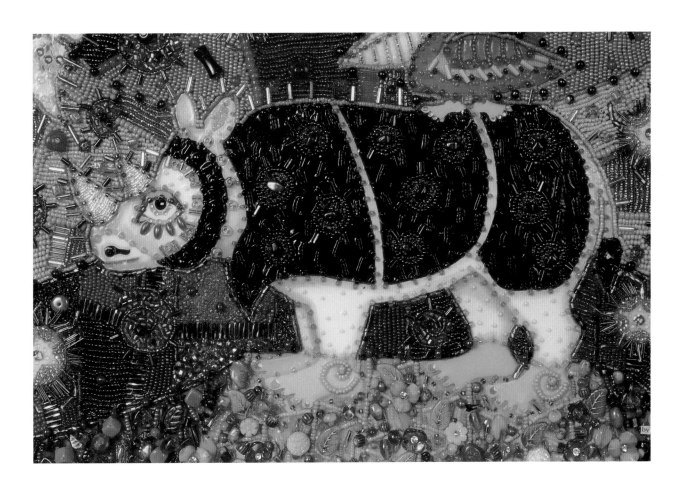

My work consists of small, intimate paintings and objects embellished with beads and found objects. I have a compulsive need to fill each piece with this three-dimensional detail. The subject matter in the paintings usually consists of animals, people, and mystical creatures in a setting full of color and fantasy. There is both a light whimsical effect to this work as well as a deeper quality operating through the symbolic narrative of mythology, dreams, and imagination. This work has become a constant source of discovery for me because the narrative element it contains helps me identify meaning in my life.

Nancy Zellers
Aurora, Colorado
Malignant Paradise

What a feeling of betrayal when one of these apples of pride and pleasure turns out to be rotten at the core. Although breast cancer was the second time I had cancer, it felt the most invasive and was more emotionally disturbing. A real loss of innocence regarding my immortality and invulnerability accompanied breast cancer.

This piece, *Malignant Paradise*, is a reflection of that feeling. My innocent paradise was destroyed. Things will never be the same. There was a worm/snake in my apple.

Show Itinerary

Bead International 2000 will be on display at the Dairy Barn Cultural Arts Center from May 27–September 3, 2000. A portion of the exhibit will then travel to various host venues. If you would like to see *Bead International 2000* in your area, please encourage your local museum or gallery to contact The Dairy Barn to request information about the touring exhibit.

November–December 2000
Mitchell Museum at Cedarhurst
Mt. Vernon, Illinois

February–March 2001
Pratt Museum
Homer, Alaska

May–June 2001
Holland Area Arts Council
Holland, Michigan

September–October 2001 *Tentative*
Museum in the Community
Hurricane, West Virginia

About The Dairy Barn

The Dairy Barn Southeastern Ohio Cultural Arts Center, located in the Appalachian foothills, features a full, year-round calendar of exhibits, special activities, and arts education classes for children and adults. The mission of the Dairy Barn is to promote regional, national, and international arts, crafts, and cultural heritage in Southeastern Ohio, through exhibitions and programs that are unique, educational, family-oriented, and fun.

The history of the Dairy Barn is as colorful as its exhibits. Built in 1913, the structure housed an active dairy herd until the late 1960s. Ten years later, local arts enthusiasts Harriet and Ora Anderson recognized the building's potential as a much-needed regional arts center, and they worked tirelessly to rally community support to save the unused, dilapidated structure. The rescue occurred only nine days before the scheduled demolition! Placed on the National Register of Historic Places, the building became the Dairy Barn Southeastern Ohio Cultural Arts Center.

The architects retained the original character of the building as several renovations turned it from a seasonal, makeshift exhibit space into a first-class, fully accessible arts facility with a 6,500 square foot gallery and the specially equipped Ann Howland Arts Education Center. A $1.5 million renovation and expansion project to make the facility a full-service arts center is currently in progress. When this project is completed in the year 2000, the Barn will have five new classrooms, a catering area, and a gift shop.

The Dairy Barn is supported by admissions, memberships, corporate sponsorships, grants, and donations. The staff is assisted by a large group of volunteers who annually donate thousands of hours of time and talent. For a calendar of events and information about Dairy Barn programs, contact the Dairy Barn Arts Center, P.O Box 747, Athens, OH 45701; phone 740-592-4981; fax 740-592-5090; email info@dairybarn.org; or visit the website at www.dairybarn.org.

About *Beadwork*

OVER 10 GREAT PROJECTS PLUS IMPORTANT BEAD INFO!

March/April 2000 issue featuring the work of bead artist Marcus Amerman. *Samuel American Horse, 1999.*

Beadwork magazine is the latest achievement in Interweave Press's 25 years of craft publishing. First introduced in 1996 as a special issue, *Beadwork* has been publishing quarterly since 1998 with editor Jean Campbell at the helm.

The magazine is devoted to every kind of bead stitching and creating. Its pages are filled with the latest innovations of the craft, including seed bead stitching, wirework, lampwork, and bead knitting, crochet, and embroidery. *Beadwork* features beautiful photographs and drawings that illustrate projects designed by beadworkers all over the world. Its artist profiles, tips, calendar, and reviews allow readers to keep their fingers on the pulse of the international bead community.

Since 1998 *Beadwork* editor Jean Campbell has become a major figure in the bead world. She is the co-author of the best-selling book, *The Beader's Companion.* She has been asked to be a juror in the Third International Miyuki Beadwork Challenge. *Beadwork's* annual "Bead Bash" and contests attract hundreds of this country's best beadworkers. Jean knows exactly what beadworkers want, and she gives it to them in *Beadwork* magazine. In fact, the magazine is so popular that it's recently gone from four to six issues a year.

Beadwork began a line of how-to bead books in 1998 with *The Beader's Companion*, a concise, user-friendly book that details beading techniques. It has sold over 16,000 copies. Now in its second printing, *Beading on a Loom* by Don Pierce is a comprehensive book that covers all aspects of contemporary and historic loomweaving. *Beading with Peyote Stitch* by Jeannette Cook and Vicki Star is the third in *Beadwork*'s line with easy step-by-step instructions and a beautiful gallery of this popular stitch. Upcoming *Beadwork* books include *All Wired Up: Wire Techniques for the Beadworker and Jewelry Maker* by Mark Lareau, available in fall 2000, and a book on brick stitch by Diane Fitzgerald, available in early 2001.

All Wired Up: Wire Techniques for the Beadworker & Jewelry Maker
Mark Lareau
8½ × 9, paperback, 128 pages.
#1029—$21.95

Beading with Peyote Stitch
Jeannette Cook & Vicki Star
8½ × 9, paperbound,
112 pages. #1018—$21.95

Beading on a Loom
Don Pierce
8½ × 9, paperbound, 112 pages.
#1027—$21.95

The Beader's Companion
Judith Durant & Jean Campbell
7 × 5, spiral-bound, 112 pages.
#671—$19.95

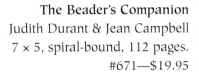

Call today for more information on our complete selection of books: 800-272-2193
Interweave Press, 201 E. Fourth Street, Loveland, CO 80537-5655 • www.interweave.com

page 101

page 92